The White Peacock

and Other Works for Solo Piano

CHARLES TOMLINSON GRIFFES

DOVER PUBLICATIONS, INC.
Mineola, New York

Published in Canada by General Publishing Company, Ltd., 30 Lesmill Road, Don Mills, Toronto, Ontario.
Published in the United Kingdom by Constable and Company, Ltd., 3 The Lanchesters, 162–164 Fulham Palace Road, London W6 9ER.

Bibliographical Note

This Dover edition, first published in 1999, is a new compilation of the following works, originally published separately by G. Schirmer, New York: *Charles T. Griffes / Op. 5: Three Tone-Pictures,* 1915; *Op. 6: Fantasy Pieces,* 1915; *Op. 7: Roman Sketches,* 1917; *Sonata,* 1921.

Epigraphs are now grouped at the beginning of each suite of pieces; they originally appeared individually, either above the first system of music or on a facing page.

International Standard Book Number: 0-486-40406-4

Manufactured in the United States of America
Dover Publications, Inc., 31 East 2nd Street, Mineola, N.Y. 11501

Contents

The White Peacock

and Other Works for Solo Piano

Three Tone-Pictures

Op. 5

Epigraphs to

THREE TONE-PICTURES
Op. 5

(The Lake at Evening)

. . . for always . . .
I hear lake water lapping with low sounds
by the shore . . .

William Butler Yeats
From *The Lake Isle of Innisfree*

(The Vale of Dreams)

At midnight, in the month of June,
I stand beneath the mystic moon.
An opiate vapour, dewy, dim,
Exhales from out her golden rim,
And, softly dripping, drop by drop,
Upon the quiet mountain top,
Steals drowsily and musically
Into the universal valley.

Edgar Allan Poe
From *The Sleeper*

(The Night Winds)

But when the Night had thrown her pall
Upon that spot, as upon all,
And the mystic wind went by
Murmuring in melody—
Then—ah then I would awake
To the terror of the lone lake.

Edgar Allan Poe
From *The Lake: To—*

To Leslie Hodgson

The Lake at Evening

Op. 5, No. 1 (1910, later revised)

più espressivo
mp
tre corde
p
p
mf
poco agitato
sempre cresc.
f
p
più tranquillo
dim. molto
poco rit.

Tempo I°
pp
una corda
Ped.
Ped.
Ped.
Ped.
8
pp
Ped.
Ped.
Ped.
8
sempre dim. e
p
lontano
pp
Ped.
Ped.
8
più calmato
ppp
morendo
Ped.
Ped.

The Vale of Dreams

Op. 5, No. 2 (ca. 1912)

dim.
pp
ppp
mf
inquietamente
dim.
p
cresc.
molto cresc. e agitato

8
f
dim. molto
p
pp tranquillo
ppp
Tempo Iº
p
sempre pp
3
poco marcato

poco marcato
p
pp
dim.
pp
8
8
p dim.
ppp
Ped.

The Night Winds

Op. 5, No. 3 (1912)

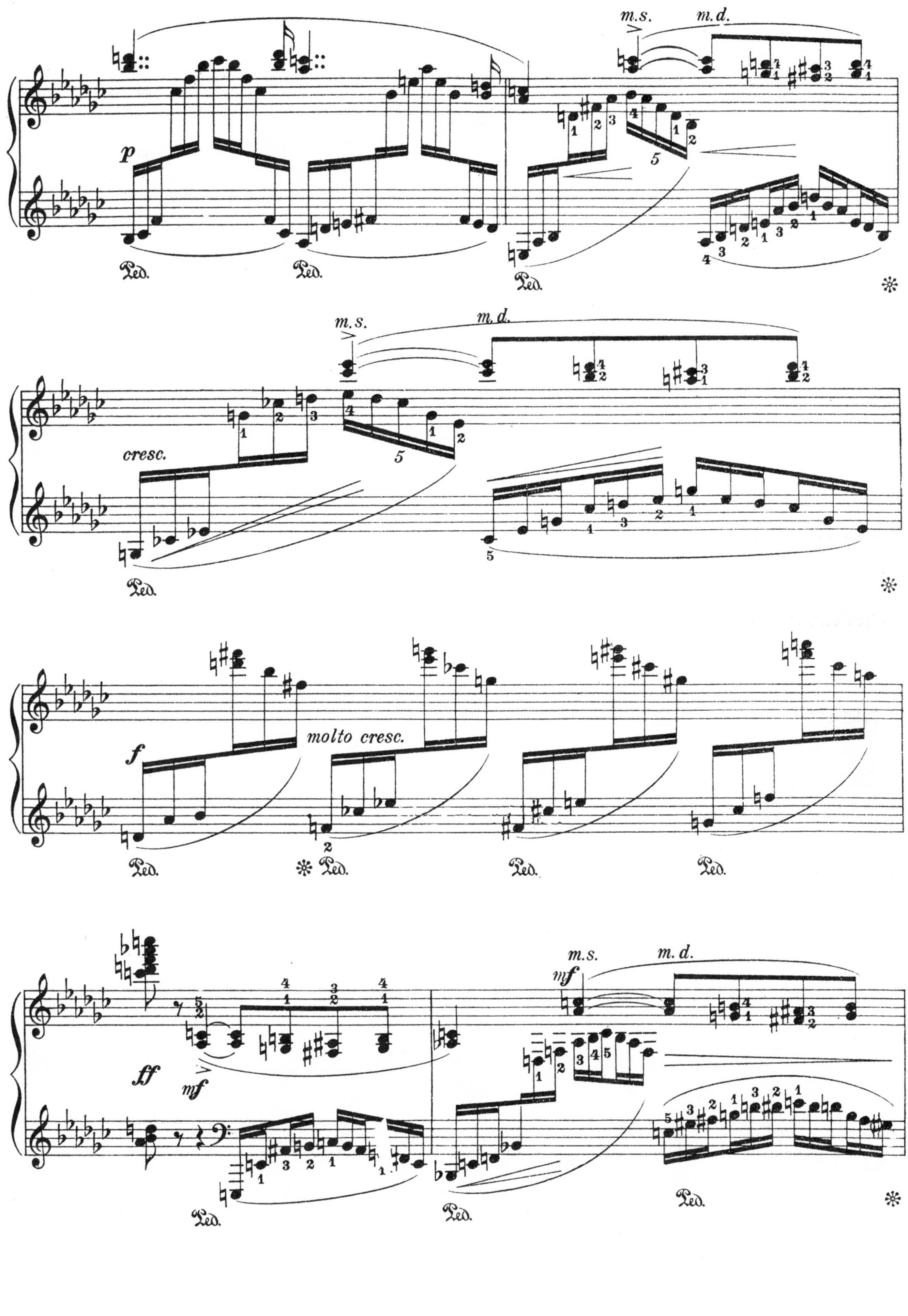
m.s.
m.d.
p
Ped.
cresc.
molto cresc.
f
ff
mf

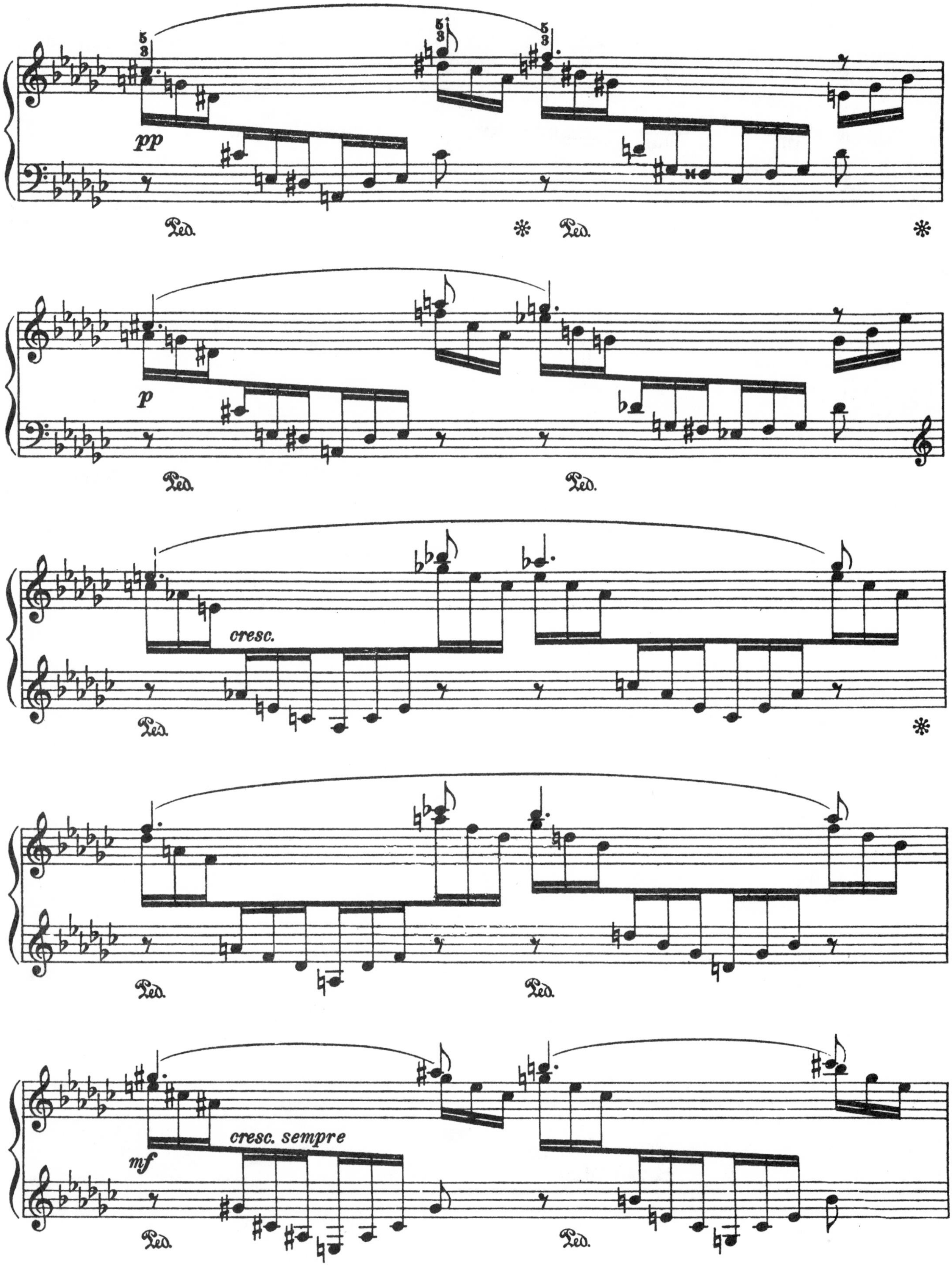
pp
Ped.
p
cresc.
cresc. sempre
mf

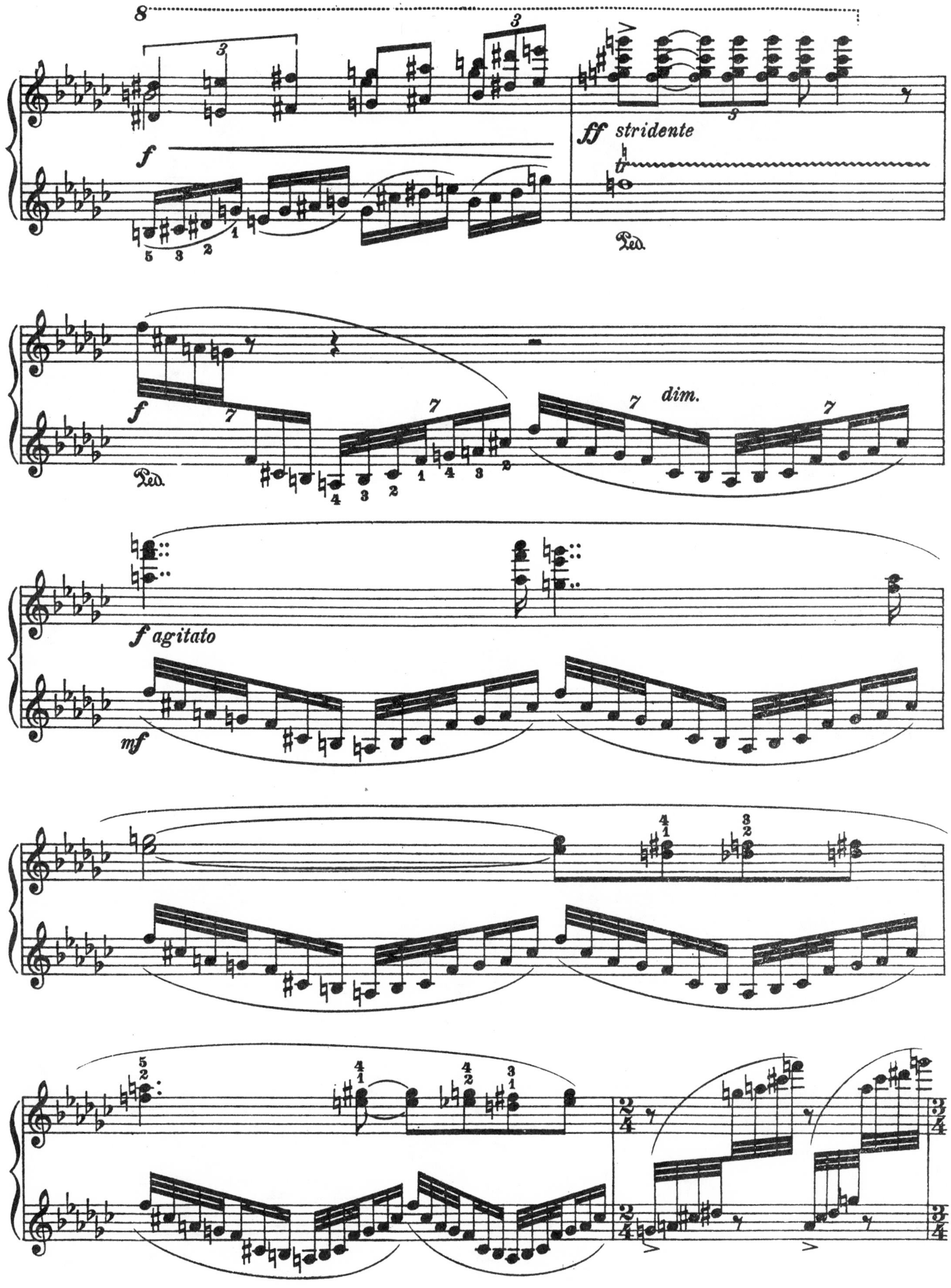
f
ff stridente
Ped.
f
dim.
Ped.
f agitato
mf

8
resc. molto
8
stridente
ff
9
sf
mf
p calmando
pp
pp
misterioso
Ped.
Ped.
Ped.
Ped.
quasi da lontano
pp
3
una corda
pp
Ped.

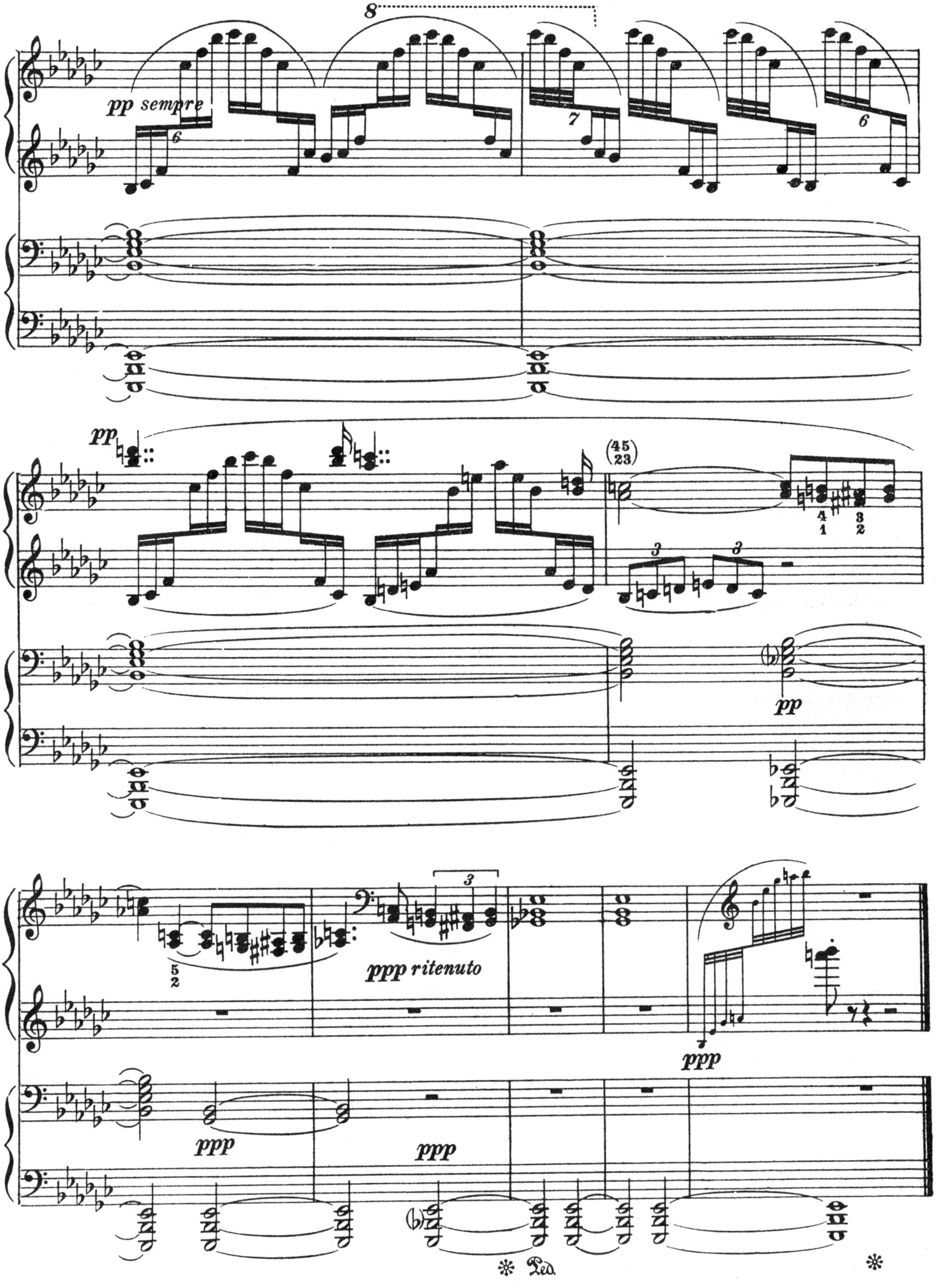
pp sempre
pp
pp
ppp
ppp ritenuto
ppp
ppp
Ped.

Fantasy Pieces

Op. 6

Epigraphs to

FANTASY PIECES

Op. 6

[Barcarolle]

. . . the old impetuous sea
Changeless, yet full of change, it seems
The very mirror of those dreams
We call men's lives—
. . . .
As . . . one great wave
Doth rise and scorn an ocean-grave,
And leaves its crown of foam where high
The cliffs stare seaward steadily:
So from love's throbbing, pulsing sea
All lightning-lit by passion, reared
A might wave resistlessly.

William Sharp*

[Notturno]

L'étang reflète,	*The pool reflects,*
Profond miroir,	*Deep mirror,*
La silhouette	*The silhouette*
Du saule noir	*Of the black willow*
Où le vent pleure . . .	*Where the wind cries . . .*
Rêvons; c'est l'heure.	*Let us dream; it's time.*

Paul Verlaine

[Scherzo]

From the Palace of Enchantment there issued into the night sounds of unearthly revelry. Troops of genii and other fantastic spirits danced grotesquely to a music now weird and mysterious, now wild and joyous.

[uncredited]

*Scottish poet and man of letters, William Sharp—secretly publishing under the name "Fiona Macleod" after 1894—was one of the leading figures in the Celtic renaissance of the late 19th century.

To Gottfried Galston

Barcarolle

Op. 6, No. 1 (1912)

mf molto espressivo
p
f

p la melodia
pp
pp l'accompagnamento
Ped.
Ped. simile
mf
cresc. sempre
p
mf
cresc.
f
Ped.

con passione
f
f
cresc.
ff
dim.
leggiero
p
dim.
pp
ppp
poco rit.

tranquillamente
p
ppp
poco
pp sempre
Ped.
poco cresc.
dim.
f
animato
mf

più animato e forte
Ped.
ff
f
dim. molto
dim.
poco rit.
ppp calmato

p espressivo
Ped.
pp
languendo
poco cresc.

poco cresc.
poco cresc.
Ped.
poco cresc.
pp
rit.
Tempo I°
pp ma poco marcato
m.d. m.s.
pp
espressivo
pp

cantabile
Ped.
cresc.
f
p

cresc.
dim.
Ped. simile
f
Ped.
8
f
cresc. molto
Ped.

poco più animato e trionfante
8
ff
Ped.
Ped.
Ped.
Ped.
Ped.
8
sempre ff e più animato
Ped.
Ped.
Ped.
Ped.
Ped.
cresc. molto e precipitoso

trionfante, non affrettato
ff
f
Ped.
affrettato
ff
sf
accelerando
Ped.
f
Ped.
8
ff

Notturno

Op. 6, No. 2 (1915)

mf
cresc.
f
cresc. sempre
ff
dim.
p
dim.
pp
rit.
Ped.

sognando
pp
Ped.

pp calmato
pp
Ped.
pp
mf
poco cresc.
cresc. sempre
ff
f

p
cresc.
f
molto dim. e rit.
Meno mosso
lontano
pp
molto cantabile
mf tranquillo
più rit.

poco agitato
cresc.
f
più agitato
f poco a poco calmato e dim.

Tempo I°
pp mormorando
Ped.
p
Ped.
Ped.
mf
Ped.
p
dim.
Ped.

mf
Ped.
mf
cresc. sempre
f
cresc. sempre
ff
dim. sempre
pp

pp tranquillo
dolce, ma espressivo
p
molto dim.
pp
Ped.

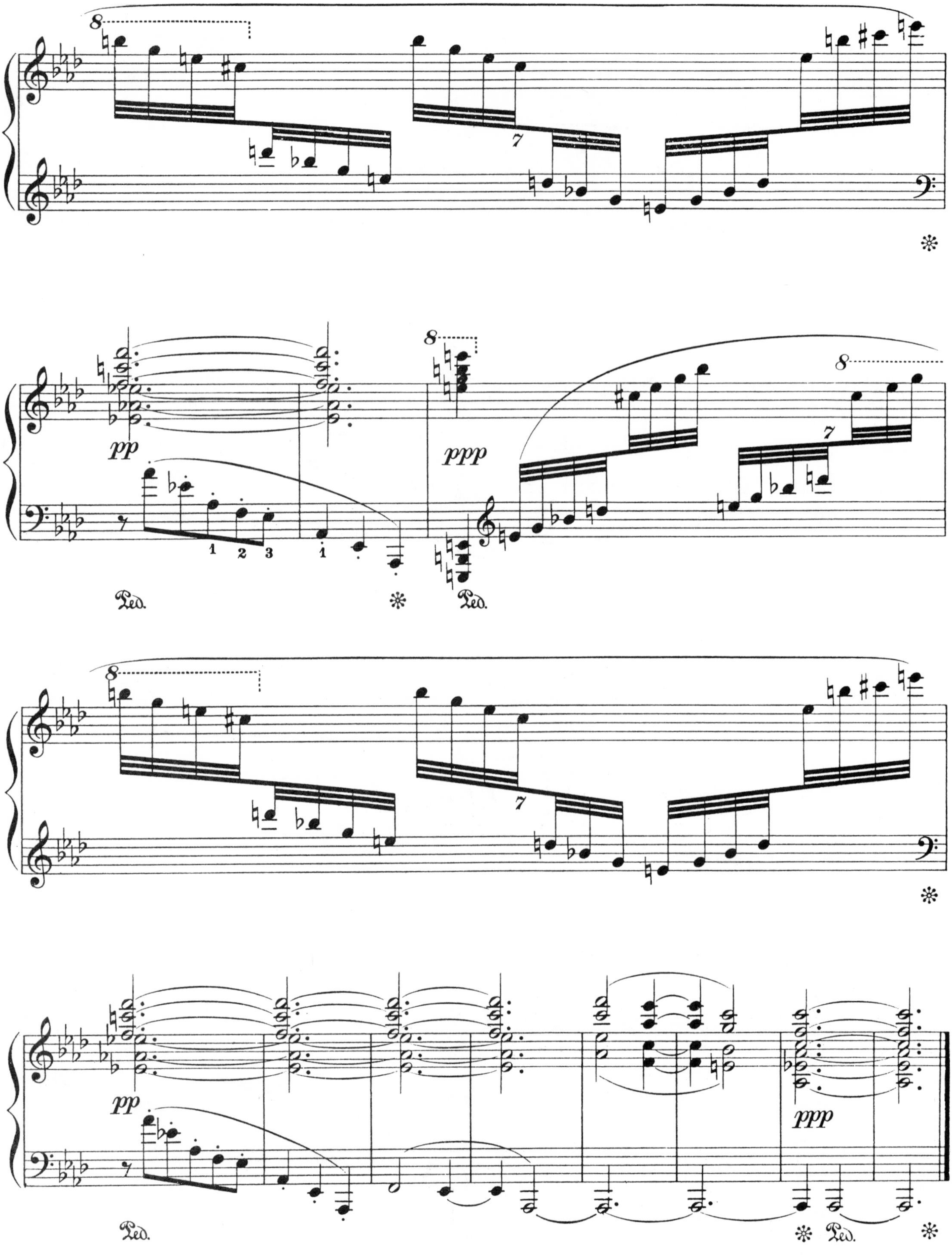

8
7
8
pp
ppp
8
7
1
2
3
1
Ped.
Ped.
8
7
pp
ppp
Ped.
Ped.

Scherzo

Op. 6, No. 3 (1913)

(orchestrated as "Bacchanale," ca. 1919)

f
f gioioso
Ped.
ff
mf
pp
scherzando

pp
Ped.
cresc.
ff
Ped.
ff
f
dim. molto
pp misterioso
Ped. una corda
Ped.

cresc.
f marc.
sempre cresc.
ff marc.
ed accel.
ff
a tempo
marcato
sf
mf

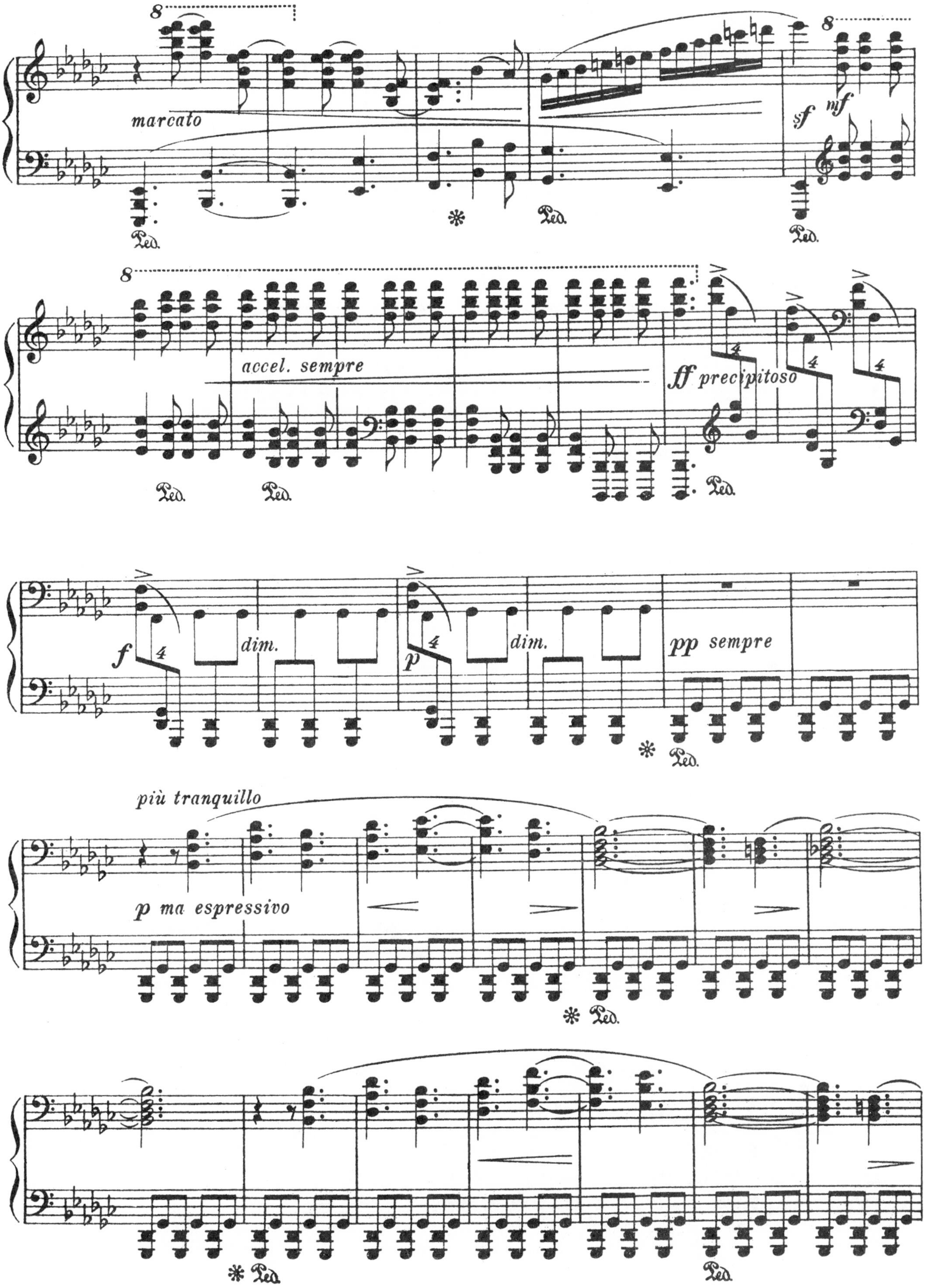
marcato
sf
mf
accel. sempre
ff precipitoso
f
dim.
p
dim.
pp sempre
più tranquillo
p ma espressivo

pp
pp
pp

Poco meno mosso
pp
espressivo
p
cresc.
pp
Ped.
Ped.
Ped. simile
mf
dim.
p
cresc.

p
f
p
dim.
pp
p
pp
p
perdendosi
pp lontano
rit.
poco a poco tornando al tempo del principio
pp

p
sf
mf
f gioioso

f
f
ff
mf
pp scherzando
cresc.
cresc. molto
ff

poco meno mosso
f
Ped.
Ped. simile
poco a
cresc.
poco più animato
Ped.

ff
ff con fuoco
Ped.
sf
ff sempre accel.
precipitato
8
furioso
f
ff

Roman Sketches

Op. 7

Epigraphs to

ROMAN SKETCHES

Op. 7

Poems are by William Sharp, from his *Sospiri di Roma* (1891).

(**The White Peacock**)

. . . Here where the sunlight
Floodeth the garden,
Where the pomegranate
Reareth its glory
Of gorgeous blossom;
Where the oleanders
Dream through the noontides;

. . . .

. . . Where the heat lies
Pale blue in the hollows,

. . . .

Here where the dream-flowers,
The cream-white poppies,
Silently waver,

. . . .

Here as the breath, as the soul of this beauty
Moveth in silence, and dreamlike, and slowly,
White as a snowdrift in mountain valleys
When softly upon it the gold light lingers:

. . . .

Moves the white peacock, as tho' through the noontide
A dream of the moonlight were real for a moment.
Dim on the beautiful fan that he spreadeth,

. . . .

Dim on the cream-white are blue adumbrations,

. . . .

Pale, pale as the breath of blue smoke in far woodlands,
Here, as the breath, as the soul of this beauty,
Moves the White Peacock.

(**Nightfall**)

The long day is over.
Dusk, and silence now:
And night, that is dew
On the flower of the World.

(**The Fountain of the Acqua Paola**)

Shimmering lights,
As though the Aurora's
Wild polar fires
Flashed in thy happy bubbles,
Died in thy foam.

(**Clouds**)

Mountainous glories,
They move superbly;
Crumbling so slowly,
That none perceives when
The golden domes
Are sunk in the valleys
Of fathomless snows.

To Rudolph Ganz

The White Peacock

Op. 7, No. 1 (1915)

Languidamente e molto rubato
una corda

poco cresc.
pp
3
3
5
5
Con languore
p
poco affrett.

p esitando
affrett.
mf
f
affrett.
f dim.
p tranquillo

cresc.
dim.
p
mf
pp
7
p
pp

p
cresc.
mf
cresc.
8
f
cresc.
ff

pp
p
mf
ppp
7
3
molto dim. e rit.

To Winifred Christie

Nightfall

Al far della notte

Op. 7, No. 2 (1916)

p
p
mf accel. e cresc.
tre corde
pp
p
f
mf rubato
cresc.
dim. e rit.

pp
3
pp poco a poco più mosso
mf
mf
f

(♩= 138)
8
f
8
molto cresc.
3
p
8
ff
gliss.
p
trillo ad lib.
8
f senza dim.
ff

Tranquillo (♩= 54-56)
f > pp
pp
p
mf
dim.
pp una corda

pp
pp
dim.
tre corde
p espress.
pp
p
p
p
f
molto cresc.

ff
f
mf
rubato
cresc.
mf
dim.
rit.
p
pp
mf

p
tr
Tempo I°
pp una corda
p
dim.
ppp
pp
p
ppp
pp
pppp
ppp
3
pp
pp e molto rit.
ppp

The Fountain of the Acqua Paola

Op. 7, No. 3 (1916)

8
mf
poco rit.
Meno mosso
p rubato
pp
pp
pp
pp

pp
pp
f
Più animato
f
f

Calmato (♩= circa 108)
p
mf
dim. e poco rit.
a tempo
pp

cresc. e accel.
mf
sempre cresc.
8
f
dim.
rit.

a tempo
8
f
5
8
5
Agitato
mf

molto appassionato
f
ff
8
ff
3
molto dim.

Tempo I°
pp
p espressivo
8

8
p
3
pp
una corda
p
pp
dim.
ppp rit.

To Mr. Paul Rosenfeld

Clouds

Op. 7, No. 4 (1916)

p
dim.
non troppo lento
pp
pp

Più mosso
p
mf
cresc.
8
f
p
cresc. e poco accel.
pp
una corda

Più tranquillo
espressivo
mf
tre corde
poco agitato e cresc.
f

Tempo I°
8
p
8
sempre dim.
8
pp quasi lontano
pp

pp
pp
ppp
ppp
rit.
rit.

Sonata

To Rudolph Ganz

Sonata

(1917–18, revised 1919)

mf
cresc.
p
mf
cresc.
f
mf dim.
p

mf
f marcato
cresc.
ff
p
mf
f
mf
f

8
cresc.
3
5
5
5
5
8
2
4
f
4
5
4
5
5
marcato
8
2
4
f
5
4
f
cresc.
5
f
ff

8
f
8
f
mf
molto dim.
8
pp
mf espressivo
pp
4
4

mf
f

accel.
f
8
ff
mf
dim. e rit.
Tempo I°
flebile
pp
pp
Ped.
3
tr
f
pp
Ped.

p
f
mf
p
cresc.
p
p

f
mf
f marcato
f
p
f
p
f
f
dim.
p espressivo

mf
f
8
sempre cresc.

agitato molto
mf
cresc.
f
p
mf
p
cresc.
f
mf
f

cresc.
marcato
poco agitato
dim.
dim. e rit.

Tranquillamente
espressivo
cresc.

ff
sempre ff
mf
molto cresc.
ff
Ped. sempre
mf
dim.
p
pp rit.
Molto tranquillo
p espressivo
pp

p
mf
espressivo
mf
p
pp
mf
rit.
mf

a tempo
marcato
poco agitato
dim.

appassionato
accel.
pp rit.
tranquillo
dim.

pp
molto rit.
pp
p
accel.
f sempre accel.
f
8

Allegro vivace
p
p
mf
marcato
f
8
8
f
8
f

8
f
ff
f
p
mf
f
8
p
8
p
mf
mf

8
f
ff
sempre ff
mf
f marcato
f
f
ff

cresc.

Appassionato
8
f
8
f
f
f
cresc.
8

ritardando
meno mosso
ff
p
p
pp
p
p
dim.
rit.
quasi timpani

Lento
pp misterioso
pp
p
p
p
mf
mf
f
f
8
8
cresc.
ff

Tempo primo
pp poco a poco molto vivace
p
mf
8
f

Presto
8
f
8
mf

END OF EDITION

Dover Piano and Keyboard Editions

SHORTER WORKS FOR PIANOFORTE SOLO, Franz Schubert. All piano music except Sonatas, Dances, and a few unfinished pieces. Contains Wanderer, Impromptus, Moments Musicals, Variations, Scherzi, etc. Breitkopf and Härtel edition. 199pp. 9⅜ × 12¼. 22648-4 Pa. **$11.95**

WALTZES AND SCHERZOS, Frédéric Chopin. All of the Scherzos and nearly all (20) of the Waltzes from the authoritative Mikuli edition. Editorial commentary. 160pp. 9 × 12. 24316-8 Pa. **$9.95**

COMPLETE PRELUDES AND ETUDES FOR SOLO PIANO, Frédéric Chopin. All 25 Preludes, all 27 Etudes by greatest composer of piano music. Authoritative Mikuli edition. 192pp. 9 × 12. 24052-5 Pa. **$8.95**

COMPLETE BALLADES, IMPROMPTUS AND SONATAS, Frédéric Chopin. The four Ballades, four Impromptus and three Sonatas. Authoritative Paderewski edition. 240pp. 9 × 12. (Available in U.S. only) 24164-5 Pa. **$10.95**

NOCTURNES AND POLONAISES, Frédéric Chopin. 20 *Nocturnes* and 11 *Polonaises* reproduced from the authoritative Mikuli edition for pianists, students, and musicologists. Commentary. 224pp. 9 × 12. 24564-0 Pa. **$10.95**

COMPLETE MAZURKAS, Frédéric Chopin. 51 best-loved compositions, reproduced directly from the authoritative Kistner edition edited by Carl Mikuli. 160pp. 9 × 12. 25548-4 Pa. **$8.95**

FANTASY IN F MINOR, BARCAROLLE, BERCEUSE AND OTHER WORKS FOR SOLO PIANO, Frédéric Chopin. 15 works, including one of the greatest of the Romantic period, the Fantasy in F Minor, Op. 49, reprinted from the authoritative German edition prepared by Chopin's student, Carl Mikuli. 224pp. 8⅜ × 11¼. 25950-1 Pa. **$7.95**

COMPLETE HUNGARIAN RHAPSODIES FOR SOLO PIANO, Franz Liszt. All 19 Rhapsodies reproduced directly from an authoritative Russian edition. All headings, footnotes translated to English. Best one volume edition available. 224pp. 8⅜ × 11¼. 24744-9 Pa. **$11.95**

ANNÉES DE PÈLERINAGE, COMPLETE, Franz Liszt. Authoritative Russian edition of piano masterpieces: *Première Année (Suisse): Deuxième Année (Italie)* and *Venezia e Napoli; Troisième Année,* other related pieces. 288pp. 9⅜ × 12¼. 25627-8 Pa. **$13.95**

COMPLETE ETUDES FOR SOLO PIANO, Series I: Including the Transcendental Etudes, Franz Liszt, edited by Busoni. Also includes Etude in 12 Exercises, 12 Grandes Etudes and Mazeppa. Breitkopf & Härtel edition. 272pp. 8⅜ × 11¼. 25815-7 Pa. **$12.95**

COMPLETE ETUDES FOR SOLO PIANO, Series II: Including the Paganini Etudes and Concert Etudes, Franz Liszt, edited by Busoni. Also includes Morceau de Salon, Ab Irato. Breitkopf & Härtel edition. 192pp. 8⅜ × 11¼. 25816-5 Pa. **$9.95**

SONATA IN B MINOR AND OTHER WORKS FOR PIANO, Franz Liszt. One of Liszt's most performed piano masterpieces, with the six Consolations, ten *Harmonies poetiques et religieuses,* two Ballades and two Legendes. Breitkopf & Härtel edition. 208pp. 8⅜ × 11¼. 26182-4 Pa. **$9.95**

PIANO TRANSCRIPTIONS FROM FRENCH AND ITALIAN OPERAS, Franz Liszt. Virtuoso transformations of themes by Mozart, Verdi, Bellini, other masters, into unforgettable music for piano. Published in association with American Liszt Society. 247pp. 9 × 12. 24273-0 Pa. **$13.95**

MEPHISTO WALTZ AND OTHER WORKS FOR SOLO PIANO, Franz Liszt. Rapsodie Espagnole, Liebestraüme Nos. 1–3, Valse Oubliée No. 1, Nuages Gris, Polonaises Nos. 1 and 2, Grand Galop Chromatique, more. 192pp. 8⅜ × 11¼. 28147-7 Pa. **$10.95**

COMPLETE WORKS FOR PIANOFORTE SOLO, Felix Mendelssohn. Breitkopf and Härtel edition of Capriccio in F# Minor, Sonata in E Major, Fantasy in F# Minor, Three Caprices, Songs without Words, and 20 other works. Total of 416pp. 9⅜ × 12¼. Two-vol. set. 23136-4, 23137-2 Pa. **$23.90**

COMPLETE SONATAS AND VARIATIONS FOR SOLO PIANO, Johannes Brahms. All sonatas, five variations on themes from Schumann, Paganini, Handel, etc. Vienna Gesellschaft der Musikfreunde edition. 178pp. 9 × 12. 22650-6 Pa. **$10.95**

COMPLETE SHORTER WORKS FOR SOLO PIANO, Johannes Brahms. All solo music not in other two volumes. Waltzes, Scherzo in E Flat Minor, Eight Pieces, Rhapsodies, Fantasies, Intermezzi, etc. Vienna Gesellschaft der Musikfreunde. 180pp. 9 × 12. 22651-4 Pa. **$10.95**

COMPLETE TRANSCRIPTIONS, CADENZAS AND EXERCISES FOR SOLO PIANO, Johannes Brahms. Vienna Gesellschaft der Musikfreunde edition, vol. 15. Studies after Chopin, Weber, Bach; gigues, sarabandes; 10 Hungarian dances, etc. 178pp. 9 × 12. 22652-2 Pa. **$10.95**

PIANO MUSIC OF ROBERT SCHUMANN, Series I, edited by Clara Schumann. Major compositions from the period 1830–39; *Papillons,* Toccata, Grosse Sonate No. 1, *Phantasiestücke, Arabeske, Blumenstück,* and nine other works. Reprinted from Breitkopf & Härtel edition. 274pp. 9⅜ × 12¼. 21459-1 Pa. **$13.95**

PIANO MUSIC OF ROBERT SCHUMANN, Series II, edited by Clara Schumann. Major compositions from period 1838–53; *Humoreske, Novelletten,* Sonate No. 2, 43 *Clavierstücke für die Jugend,* and six other works. Reprinted from Breitkopf & Härtel edition. 272pp. 9⅜ × 12¼. 21461-3 Pa. **$13.95**

PIANO MUSIC OF ROBERT SCHUMANN, Series III, edited by Clara Schumann. All solo music not in other two volumes, including *Symphonic Etudes, Phantaisie,* 13 other choice works. Definitive Breitkopf & Härtel edition. 224pp. 9⅜ × 12¼. 23906-3 Pa. **$11.95**

PIANO MUSIC 1888–1905, Claude Debussy. Deux Arabesques, Suite Bergamesque, Masques, first series of Images, etc. Nine others, in corrected editions. 175pp. 9⅜ × 12¼. 22771-5 Pa. **$8.95**

COMPLETE PRELUDES, Books 1 and 2, Claude Debussy. 24 evocative works that reveal the essence of Debussy's genius for musical imagery, among them many of the composer's most famous piano compositions. Glossary of French terms. 128pp. 8⅜ × 11¼. 25970-6 Pa. **$7.95**

PRELUDES, BOOK I: The Autograph Score, Claude Debussy. Superb facsimile reproduced directly from priceless autograph score in Pierpont Morgan Library in New York. New Introduction by Roy Howat. 48pp. 8⅜ × 11. 25549-2 Pa. **$8.95**

PIANO MASTERPIECES OF MAURICE RAVEL, Maurice Ravel. Handsome affordable treasury; *Pavane pour une infante defunte, jeux d'eau, Sonatine, Miroirs,* more. 128pp. 9 × 12. (Not available in France or Germany) 25137-3 Pa. **$8.95**

COMPLETE LYRIC PIECES FOR PIANO, Edvard Grieg. All 66 pieces from Grieg's ten sets of little mood pictures for piano, favorites of generations of pianists. 224pp. 9⅜ × 12¼. 26176-X Pa. **$11.95**

*Available from your music dealer or write for **free** Music Catalog to Dover Publications, Inc., Dept. MUBI, 31 East 2nd Street, Mineola, N.Y. 11501.*

Dover Piano and Keyboard Editions

THE WELL-TEMPERED CLAVIER: Books I and II, Complete, Johann Sebastian Bach. All 48 preludes and fugues in all major and minor keys. Authoritative Bach-Gesellschaft edition. Explanation of ornaments in English, tempo indications, music corrections. 208pp. 9⅜ × 12¼. 24532-2 Pa. **$9.95**

KEYBOARD MUSIC, J. S. Bach. Bach-Gesellschaft edition. For harpsichord, piano, other keyboard instruments. English Suites, French Suites, Six Partitas, Goldberg Variations, Two-Part Inventions, Three-Part Sinfonias. 312pp. 8⅛ × 11. 22360-4 Pa. **$12.95**

ITALIAN CONCERTO, CHROMATIC FANTASIA AND FUGUE AND OTHER WORKS FOR KEYBOARD, Johann Sebastian Bach. Sixteen of Bach's best-known, most-performed and most-recorded works for the keyboard, reproduced from the authoritative Bach-Gesellschaft edition. 112pp. 9 × 12. 25387-2 Pa. **$8.95**

COMPLETE KEYBOARD TRANSCRIPTIONS OF CONCERTOS BY BAROQUE COMPOSERS, Johann Sebastian Bach. Sixteen concertos by Vivaldi, Telemann and others, transcribed for solo keyboard instruments. Bach-Gesellschaft edition. 128pp. 9⅜ × 12¼. 25529-8 Pa. **$9.95**

ORGAN MUSIC, J. S. Bach. Bach-Gesellschaft edition. 93 works. 6 Trio Sonatas, German Organ Mass, Orgelbüchlein, Six Schubler Chorales, 18 Choral Preludes. 357pp. 8⅛ × 11. 22359-0 Pa. **$13.95**

COMPLETE PRELUDES AND FUGUES FOR ORGAN, Johann Sebastian Bach. All 25 of Bach's complete sets of preludes and fugues (i.e. compositions written as pairs), from the authoritative Bach-Gesellschaft edition. 168pp. 8⅜ × 11. 24816-X Pa. **$10.95**

TOCCATAS, FANTASIAS, PASSACAGLIA AND OTHER WORKS FOR ORGAN, J. S. Bach. Over 20 best-loved works including Toccata and Fugue in D Minor, BWV 565; Passacaglia and Fugue in C Minor, BWV 582, many more. Bach-Gesellschaft edition. 176pp. 9 × 12. 25403-8 Pa. **$10.95**

TWO- AND THREE-PART INVENTIONS, J. S. Bach. Reproduction of original autograph ms. Edited by Eric Simon. 62pp. 8⅛ × 11. 21982-8 Pa. **$8.95**

THE 36 FANTASIAS FOR KEYBOARD, Georg Philipp Telemann. Graceful compositions by 18th-century master. 1923 Breslauer edition. 80pp. 8⅛ × 11. 25365-1 Pa. **$6.95**

GREAT KEYBOARD SONATAS, Carl Philipp Emanuel Bach. Comprehensive two-volume edition contains 51 sonatas by second, most important son of Johann Sebastian Bach. Originality, rich harmony, delicate workmanship. Authoritative French edition. Total of 384pp. 8⅜ × 11¼.
Series I 24853-4 Pa. **$11.95**
Series II 24854-2 Pa. **$10.95**

KEYBOARD WORKS/Series One: Ordres I–XIII; Series Two: Ordres XIV–XXVII and Miscellaneous Pieces, François Couperin. Over 200 pieces. Reproduced directly from edition prepared by Johannes Brahms and Friedrich Chrysander. Total of 496pp. 8⅛ × 11.
Series I 25795-9 Pa. **$10.95**
Series II 25796-7 Pa. **$11.95**

KEYBOARD WORKS FOR SOLO INSTRUMENTS, G. F. Handel. 35 neglected works from Handel's vast oeuvre, originally jotted down as improvisations. Includes Eight Great Suites, others. New sequence. 174pp. 9⅜ × 12¼. 24338-9 Pa. **$10.95**

WORKS FOR ORGAN AND KEYBOARD, Jan Pieterszoon Sweelinck. Nearly all of early Dutch composer's difficult-to-find keyboard works. Chorale variations; toccatas, fantasias; variations on secular, dance tunes. Also, incomplete and/or modified works, plus fantasia by John Bull. 272pp. 9 × 12. 24935-2 Pa. **$14.95**

ORGAN WORKS, Dietrich Buxtehude. Complete organ works of extremely influential pre-Bach composer. Toccatas, preludes, chorales, more. Definitive Breitkopf & Härtel edition. 320pp. 8⅜ × 11¼. (Available in U.S. only) 25682-0 Pa. **$14.95**

THE FUGUES ON THE MAGNIFICAT FOR ORGAN OR KEYBOARD, Johann Pachelbel. 94 pieces representative of Pachelbel's magnificent contribution to keyboard composition; can be played on the organ, harpsichord or piano. 100pp. 9 × 12. (Available in U.S. only) 25037-7 Pa. **$8.95**

MY LADY NEVELLS BOOKE OF VIRGINAL MUSIC, William Byrd. 42 compositions in modern notation from 1591 ms. For any keyboard instrument. 245pp. 8⅛ × 11. 22246-2 Pa. **$13.95**

ELIZABETH ROGERS HIR VIRGINALL BOOKE, edited with calligraphy by Charles J. F. Cofone. All 112 pieces from noted 1656 manuscript, most never before published. Composers include Thomas Brewer, William Byrd, Orlando Gibbons, etc. 125pp. 9 × 12. 23138-0 Pa. **$10.95**

THE FITZWILLIAM VIRGINAL BOOK, edited by J. Fuller Maitland, W. B. Squire. Famous early 17th-century collection of keyboard music, 300 works by Morley, Byrd, Bull, Gibbons, etc. Modern notation. Total of 938pp. 8⅜ × 11. Two-vol. set. 21068-5, 21069-3 Pa. **$34.90**

GREAT KEYBOARD SONATAS, Series I and Series II, Domenico Scarlatti. 78 of the most popular sonatas reproduced from the G. Ricordi edition edited by Alessandro Longo. Total of 320pp. 8⅜ × 11¼.
Series I 24996-4 Pa. **$9.95**
Series II 25003-2 Pa. **$9.95**

COMPLETE PIANO SONATAS, Joseph Haydn. 52 sonatas reprinted from authoritative Breitkopf & Härtel edition. Extremely clear and readable; ample space for notes, analysis. 464pp. 9⅜ × 12¼. 24726-0 Pa. **$11.95**
24727-9 Pa. **$11.95**

BAGATELLES, RONDOS AND OTHER SHORTER WORKS FOR PIANO, Ludwig van Beethoven. Most popular and most performed shorter works, including Rondo a capriccio in G and Andante in F. Breitkopf & Härtel edition. 128pp. 9⅜ × 12¼. 25392-9 Pa. **$8.95**

COMPLETE VARIATIONS FOR SOLO PIANO, Ludwig van Beethoven. Contains all 21 sets of Beethoven's piano variations, including the extremely popular *Diabelli Variations, Op. 120*. 240pp. 9⅜ × 12¼. 25188-8 Pa. **$12.95**

COMPLETE PIANO SONATAS, Ludwig van Beethoven. All sonatas in fine Schenker edition, with fingering, analytical material. One of best modern editions. 615pp. 9 × 12. Two-vol. set. 23134-8, 23135-6 Pa. **$25.90**

COMPLETE SONATAS FOR PIANOFORTE SOLO, Franz Schubert. All 15 sonatas. Breitkopf and Härtel edition. 293pp. 9⅜ × 12¼. 22647-6 Pa. **$13.95**

DANCES FOR SOLO PIANO, Franz Schubert. Over 350 waltzes, minuets, landler, ecossaises, other charming, melodic dance compositions reprinted from the authoritative Breitkopf & Härtel edition. 192pp. 9⅜ × 12¼. 26107-7 Pa. **$11.95**

*Available from your music dealer or write for **free** Music Catalog to Dover Publications, Inc., Dept. MUBI, 31 East 2nd Street, Mineola, N.Y. 11501.*